In a high school essay called "The Pursuit of Happiness," Dave wrote, "My restaurant would serve great tasting hamburgers made just the way you like them."

Growing Up

Dave and his father moved around a lot as Rex worked various jobs. Rex also got remarried. But two and a half years later, he and his wife, Marie, divorced. Dave and his dad were on their own again. At one point, they lived in a rooming house in Detroit, Michigan. They ate out every day.

Dave's favorite place was a hamburger stand. He liked his hamburgers with mustard, pickle, and onions. He ordered thick milkshakes on the side. The smell of hamburgers cooking made his mouth water. He would remember this place and its food when he finally got to open Wendy's many years later.

Moving was tough. Dave always had to make new friends. He never had a home base. Yet one family member could always be counted on. Dave spent summers with his grandma Minnie Sinclair in Augusta, Michigan. Grandma Minnie often said not to cut corners. She taught Dave respect, kindness, and the benefit of hard work.

Grandma Minnie put her values into action in her own restaurant job. During her shifts, Dave sat in the kitchen. Waitresses, cooks, and dishwashers rushed around. As a team, they prepared

Food Dudes

DAVE THOMAS:

Wendy's Founder

Sheila Griffin Llanas

Checkerboard Library

An Imprint of Abdo Publishing
www.abdopublishing.com

www.abdopublishing.com

Published by Abdo Publishing, a division of ABDO, PO Box 398166, Minneapolis, MN 55439. Copyright © 2015 by Abdo Consulting Group, Inc. International copyrights reserved in all countries. No part of this book may be reproduced in any form without written permission from the publisher. Checkerboard Library™ is a trademark and logo of Abdo Publishing.

Printed in the United States of America, North Mankato, Minnesota.
052014
092014

Cover Photos: Alamy, AP Images
Interior Photos: Alamy pp. 17, 27; AP Images pp. 1, 5, 11, 16, 18, 22; Getty Images pp. 19, 27

Courtesy of Wendy's. TM & ©2014 Oldemark LLC. Images used with permission. pp. 7, 8, 9, 10, 13, 15, 21, 23, 25

Series Coordinator: Megan M. Gunderson
Editor: Bridget O'Brien
Art Direction: Neil Klinepier

Library of Congress Cataloging-in-Publication Data

Llanas, Sheila Griffin, 1958- author.
  Dave Thomas : Wendy's founder / Sheila Griffin Llanas.
    pages cm. -- (Food dudes)
  Audience: Ages 9-12.
  ISBN 978-1-62403-319-3
1. Thomas, Dave, 1932-2002--Juvenile literature. 2. Wendy's International--History--Juvenile literature. 3. Restaurateurs--United States--Biography--Juvenile literature. 4. Businessmen--United States--Biography--Juvenile literature. I. Title.
  TX910.5.T56L53 2015
  647.95092--dc23
  [B]
                          2014001421

Contents

Restaurant Family

Wendy's Old Fashioned Hamburgers first opened in 1969. The owner, Dave Thomas, had two goals. The first goal was to serve fresh hamburgers fast. Hamburgers were his favorite food! The second was to create a homey environment. As a kid, Thomas never had much of a family life. He had found happiness in restaurants.

Rex David "Dave" Thomas was born on July 2, 1932, in Atlantic City, New Jersey. At six weeks old, he was adopted by Rex and Auleva Thomas, who lived in Kalamazoo, Michigan. When Dave was five, Auleva died of **rheumatic fever**. After that, Dave's life was often lonely and unsettled. He and his father moved often.

The two rarely cooked at home. Instead, they ate meals in restaurants. There, the family atmosphere made Dave happy. He watched other families laugh and talk together. He ate warm, tasty foods. Best of all, he had his father all to himself.

In diners, Dave found comforts that his homelife lacked. Food became closely connected to family. By eight years old, Dave was already dreaming of one day owning his own restaurant.

platters of home-style food. The chicken and dumplings, mashed potatoes, and vegetables in butter all looked so good.

At any restaurant, Dave paid attention to service and quality. Friendly places were best. Young Dave became a restaurant expert.

Dave and Grandma Minnie

The Night Shift

Dave, age 12

Dave's father married again. His new wife, Viola, had two daughters. When Dave was 12, the family moved to Knoxville, Tennessee. This was his fourth move in six years. Each new start seemed harder. This time, instead of seeking new friends, Dave decided to find work. He had already worked at a gas station and delivered newspapers. He had been a golf caddy and a pinsetter at a bowling alley.

What Dave really wanted was a restaurant job, but he was still too young. So, he started lying about his age. He said he was 15 to get a job helping at a grocery store. Then he worked at Walgreens. He loved wearing a uniform and serving floats and sundaes at the **soda fountain**. But when his real age was found out, he was let go. Finally, he claimed to be 16 and got a job at the Regas Restaurant.

The Regas stayed open 24 hours a day. Dave waited tables in a crisp white shirt and apron. He worked 12-hour night shifts, earning 25 cents an hour. Some days, he also earned 5 dollars in tips.

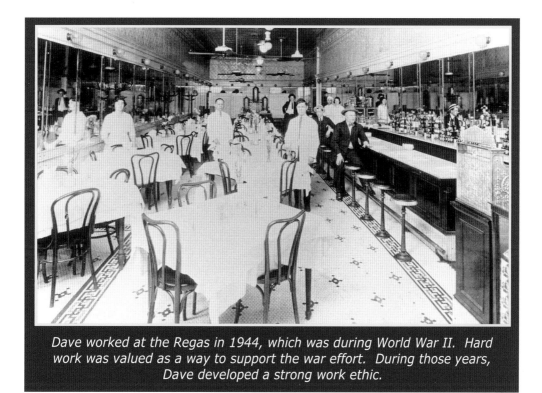

Dave worked at the Regas in 1944, which was during World War II. Hard work was valued as a way to support the war effort. During those years, Dave developed a strong work ethic.

Owners Frank and George Regas became Dave's **mentors**. The brothers looked out for their new employee. They suspected Dave was younger than he claimed. Yet determination made up for his young age. Dave loved every part of the restaurant business.

When Dave was 14, his family moved again. But, Dave gained his father's permission to stay behind. He rented a boarding house room for 7 dollars a week using his own money. Dave was crushed when his family moved one more time. He joined them in Fort Wayne, Indiana. There, he missed the Regas. The restaurant had felt like his true home.

A Shocking Truth

In 1947, Dave got another restaurant job. At the Hobby House Restaurant in Fort Wayne, he cleaned tables, mixed milkshakes, and assisted in the kitchen. The owner, Phil Clauss, became Dave's new teacher and **mentor**.

Just before this time, Grandma Minnie told Dave a secret. Dave learned that he had been adopted when he was six weeks old. His biological mother had been young and single when she put him up for adoption. This shocking news confused Dave. He felt fear and anger. Why didn't his birth mother want him? Why hadn't his adoptive father trusted him with the truth?

Soon, his father planned to move again. This time, Dave said no. He did not ask permission. He chose to stay in Fort Wayne and work at the Hobby House.

At the Hobby House, Dave tried to learn every part of the restaurant business. He knew this would be important if he ever got the chance to open his own restaurant.

At just 15 years old, Dave was working 50 hours a week. He rented a room at the YMCA a block from work. When Dave finished tenth grade, he dropped out of school. The Hobby House became his workplace and home. In 1950, 17-year-old Dave volunteered to serve in the US Army. Clauss promised Dave would still have a job when he returned home.

Dave studied the restaurant business from a very young age.
He put all he learned into his work with Wendy's.

Staff Sergeant Thomas

Even as a soldier, Thomas worked in food service. He trained in the Army Cooks and Bakers School and got a **mess hall** assignment in Germany. There, he applied his grandmother's values. He tackled tough jobs and did extra tasks. If the mess hall kitchen needed equipment, he searched for items in the garbage. On his own, he found a way to repaint the mess hall. No one told him to do the extra work. But the bright, clean look boosted **morale**.

In Germany, Thomas's roommate managed a club for soldiers. The club served simple food like cold sandwiches. But, not much was selling. Thomas had ideas to improve sales. When they worked, he was hired as an assistant. He gave tired, homesick troops better food. He added hot roast beef sandwiches, chicken-in-a-basket, and hamburgers to the menu. The place became very popular!

When Thomas returned home in October 1953, he went straight to the Hobby House. Clauss gave him a huge welcome. He met a new waitress on the staff, 18-year-old Lorraine Buskirk. Like him, Lorraine was a good worker. She had spunk! The two began to date.

Around that time, Thomas tried to locate his birth mother. He knew her name was Mollie and he found an address. But when Thomas visited, he learned that she had recently died. And soon, Thomas had a family of his own to care for. He and Lorraine married in Fort Wayne in 1954. Their first child, Pam, was born the following year.

Thomas's hard work in the army earned him a promotion to staff sergeant.

A New Mentor

One day in the mid-1950s, Colonel Harland Sanders walked into the Hobby Ranch House. This was Clauss's new restaurant, and Thomas was its general manager. Colonel Sanders was the famous owner of Kentucky Fried Chicken (KFC). When he finished eating, he invited Thomas to join him for a cup of coffee. Thomas got the feeling the conversation was important. He was right!

Clauss invested in some of the first restaurants to sell Kentucky Fried Chicken. Four **franchise** locations were in Columbus, Ohio. However, they were all failing due to poor management.

Clauss offered Thomas the tough job of improving the restaurants. Everyone warned Thomas he would fail, including Colonel Sanders. But Thomas was ready for a new challenge. In January 1962, he moved to Columbus, Ohio, and got to work.

Thomas instantly spotted more problems. The menu was too full, so he dropped unpopular items and highlighted the fried chicken. Thomas also gave each location a fresh coat of paint. He put up a cool new sign, a rotating bucket of chicken.

Thomas changed the restaurants' names to Colonel Sanders Kentucky Fried Chicken Take-Home. And to attract customers, he offered special deals and coupons. He even **bartered** with a local radio station, exchanging fried chicken for free advertising.

While Thomas worked hard in his restaurants, Lorraine cared for their five children. After Pam, they had Kenny in 1956 and Molly Jo in 1958. Wendy arrived in 1961. Lori was born in 1967. Thomas was not home very much, but his hard work was about to pay off.

Grand Opening

All four KFC locations succeeded. By 1967, Thomas was opening a fifth location. His smart business decisions included investing in KFC **stock**. In 1968, Thomas and Clauss sold their locations back to the KFC Company. The sale, plus Thomas's stock, made him a millionaire. The family splurged on a chicken-shaped swimming pool!

Soon, it was time for Thomas to pursue his lifelong dream of owning a hamburger place! In a friend's building in downtown Columbus was an empty restaurant. The friend offered that space to Thomas.

Thomas had a restaurant! Now he needed a name and a logo. His eight-year-old daughter Wendy was the picture of cute. So, he created a logo based on her. He named his hamburger place Wendy's after her, too.

Wendy had red hair and freckles. Thomas loved her happy, wholesome image.

The original Wendy's was in the first floor of this building in Columbus, Ohio.

On November 15, 1969, Thomas held the grand opening. That day, Wendy's Old Fashioned Hamburgers was packed! Even the mayor showed up. The staff dressed in crisp, white uniforms. Pretty lamps, bentwood chairs, and newsprint tabletops added a homey atmosphere.

The top menu item was made-to-order hamburgers. Wendy's also offered chili, french fries, soft drinks, and Frostys. The food, service, and décor represented old-fashioned traditions. It was exactly the family-style restaurant Thomas had dreamed of opening.

Fresh & Fast

Wendy's restaurants are still known for their famous Pick-Up Window drive-through service.

Thomas served the kind of food that he liked to eat. His food had to be served fresh and fast. At the time, a lot of fast food was fast but not fresh. Instead, pre-cooked foods were kept warm under heat lamps. Thomas was a pioneer. At Wendy's, the fresh hamburgers were square, not round. Just like Grandma Minnie had taught him so many years ago, he didn't cut corners!

Thomas had high standards. Service was good and fast. Food was fresh and fast. The hamburgers were made from fresh beef, not frozen. They took four minutes to cook. They had to be served to customers hot, fresh, and fast from the grill. Customers also got their choice of fresh toppings.

Thomas also created the Wendy's Frosty himself. He based it on the milkshakes he drank in Detroit as a kid. He mixed chocolate and vanilla ice cream. He added flavors until it tasted just right. It had to be so thick you could eat it with a spoon!

Thomas's vision caught on fast. In November 1970, Thomas opened his second Wendy's. He built it outside of town to test whether it would work in the **suburbs**. The new place, featuring a Pick-Up Window, succeeded.

The Frosty remains a popular Wendy's menu item. Today, it is available in more than just the original chocolate flavor.

In 1971, he tested other neighborhoods with two more stores. Then, he opened a Wendy's outside of Ohio, in Indiana. All the locations were popular.

Industry Honors

In August 1973, Thomas sold the first Wendy's **franchise** to L.S. Hartzog in Indianapolis, Indiana. But Thomas did not simply sell franchises for individual restaurants. He sold franchises for entire cities and regions. This idea was new in the franchise industry. It is one reason for the brand's fast success. By 1976, 500 Wendy's restaurants were up and running. The 1,500th Wendy's opened in San Juan, Puerto Rico, just three years later.

In 1979, Wendy's introduced salad bars. It was the first chain restaurant to do so. In 1983, Wendy's added another first to the menu, baked potatoes. In February 1985, the 3,000th Wendy's opened. This one was in New Orleans, Louisiana.

Thomas wanted to work less. He stepped down as CEO but remained senior chairman. But by the mid-1980s, Wendy's sales were down. At the same time, McDonald's and Burger King were fighting the "burger wars." In TV commercials, each chain claimed its hamburgers were better than the other's. Thomas did not want to put down another business in the company's national ads. He wanted to draw customers into Wendy's by providing good food and good service.

In 1979, Thomas received the Horatio Alger Award. He was
honored as a pioneer in the restaurant industry.

TV Star

In 1984, Clara Peller won an award for her TV commercial performance. Wendy's won, too. They won more customers!

With national advertising, Wendy's created a sensation. In 1984, three words became a popular catchphrase. In the commercials, three older women looked at an oversized hamburger bun with a tiny hamburger on it. Then, actress Clara Peller shouted, "Where's the beef?"

The phrase appeared on bumper stickers and T-shirts. Everyone asked, "Where's the beef?" Everyone knew the ad! And everyone knew that a square Wendy's hamburger spilled out of its bun. The ad worked to promote Wendy's quantity and quality at a competitive price.

Advertising was key to the company's success. In 1989, Thomas became a television spokesperson for his company. A single 30-second ad could take 10 hours to film. But in the end, Thomas's commercials featured his easy-going humor. The simple quality

Thomas won the Guinness World Record for Longest Running Television Advertising Campaign Starring a Company Founder.

made them enormously popular. Colonel Sanders was known nationally as the KFC founder. Thomas was now a public figure, too.

Over nearly 13 years, Thomas appeared in more than 800 Wendy's TV commercials. Thomas treated his filming crews like family, but that was no surprise. Family was a long-running theme in Thomas's life. He built his company based on his desire for a family feeling. And he treated everyone close to him like family.

Giving Back

Thomas soon championed another important family issue, adoption. Growing up, he rarely talked about being adopted. However, President George H.W. Bush requested Thomas's help. The president asked Thomas to raise awareness about adoption. Thomas realized that sharing his experience could help other children.

In 1992, he started the Dave Thomas Foundation for Adoption. Its mission is "Finding Forever Families for Children in **Foster Care**." The organization works to find a loving family for every child.

Over the years, that work has made a huge impact. The adoption process became easier. Congress created a bill to make adoption more affordable. Plus, Thomas traveled across the United States to draw attention to the cause of adoption and children in foster care.

It seemed like Thomas had accomplished everything. He was successful and he was giving back. Yet he had one regret. He had never finished high school. So, he worked hard to make up for that.

Thomas earned his **GED** from Coconut Creek High School in Fort Lauderdale, Florida. He and his wife attended the school prom. They were named prom king and queen!

The graduating class of 1993 voted Thomas Most Likely to Succeed.

Wendy's Today

In public, Thomas remained a popular figure. His **autobiography**, *Dave's Way*, was published in 1991. And, he appeared on every major television talk show. In 1996, he got to carry the Olympic torch through Dublin, Ohio, the home of the Wendy's world headquarters.

Behind the scenes, Thomas dealt with **cancer** for many years. He began kidney **dialysis** in early 2001. On January 8, 2002, he died of liver cancer at his home in Fort Lauderdale. He was 69 years old. Thomas and his wife had been married for 47 years. They had raised 5 children and had 17 grandchildren.

In business, Thomas had achieved his goal of making good hamburgers. At the time of his death, there were 6,000 Wendy's restaurants in the United States and Canada. Today, his multibillion dollar company and his foundation carry on his legacy.

Wendy's is listed in the top three hamburger chains with McDonald's and Burger King. New ad campaigns keep Wendy's fresh in people's minds. And new and favorite menu items continue to bring in customers.

Wendy's continues to update its look while maintaining a focus on customer service.

Lorraine and Wendy Thomas serve on the board of the Dave Thomas Foundation. Lorraine says, "Every time a child in **foster care** is given a loving, permanent home, we fulfill Dave's greatest wish." His company, his foundation, and his family keep Dave Thomas's vision alive.

Timeline

1932	On July 2, Rex David "Dave" Thomas was born in Atlantic City, New Jersey; he was adopted six weeks later.
1947	Dave began working at the Hobby House in Fort Wayne, Indiana.
1954	Thomas married Lorraine Buskirk.
1962	Thomas began revitalizing four Kentucky Fried Chicken franchises in Columbus, Ohio.
1968	Thomas sold his Kentucky Fried Chicken franchises and stock and became a millionaire.
1969	On November 15, the first Wendy's Old Fashioned Hamburgers opened in Columbus.
1973	In August, the first Wendy's franchise was sold.
1989	Thomas appeared in the first of more than 800 Wendy's television commercials.
1991	Thomas published his autobiography, *Dave's Way*.
1992	The Dave Thomas Foundation for Adoption was founded.
2002	On January 8, Dave Thomas died in Fort Lauderdale, Florida.

Burgers & More

Wendy's was the first national restaurant chain to add salad bars and baked potatoes to its menu. Wendy's has tested other fun items throughout the years.

1979 - Wendy's introduced salad bars.

1983 - Wendy's added baked potatoes to its menu.

1989 - With its Super Value Menu, Wendy's added 99¢ items to its menu.

1990 - Focusing on nutrition, the grilled chicken sandwich debuted.

1992 - Wendy's introduced Fresh Salads To Go.

1996 - Wendy's added heat to its menu with the Spicy Chicken Sandwich. Crispy Chicken Nuggets joined the Super Value Menu.

2004 - Kids' Meal Choices offered mandarin oranges instead of fries and milk instead of soda.

2006 - Wendy's introduced the Vanilla Frosty.

2008 - Chicken Go-Wraps expanded Wendy's sandwich offerings.

2010 - For the first time in 40 years, Wendy's changed its fries to offer natural-cut, sea salt fries.

Glossary

autobiography - a story of a person's life that is written by himself or herself.

barter - to trade goods or services without using money.

cancer - any of a group of often deadly diseases marked by harmful changes in the normal growth of cells. Cancer can spread and destroy healthy tissues and organs.

dialysis - a medical treatment used especially to aid the kidneys.

foster care - a system that provides supervision and a place to live outside a person's regular home.

franchise - the right granted to someone to sell a company's goods or services in a particular place. The business operating with this right is also known as a franchise.

GED - a test that measures the skills and knowledge required to graduate from high school.

mentor - a trusted adviser or guide.

mess hall - a military building used as a dining hall.

morale - the enthusiasm and loyalty a person or group feels about a task or job.

rheumatic fever (ru-MA-tihk FEE-vuhr) - a serious disease that occurs mainly in children. It is marked by fever, pain in the joints, and damage to the heart.

soda fountain - a store with a counter for preparing and serving sodas, sundaes, and ice cream.

stock - one of many equal parts a business is divided into. People who purchase stock own part of a company.

suburb - a town, village, or community just outside a city.

Websites

To learn more about Food Dudes,
visit **booklinks.abdopublishing.com**. These links are routinely monitored and updated to provide the most current information available.

Index